THE
RADIO

Richard and Louise Spilsbury

Raintree

www.raintreepublishers.co.uk
Visit our website to find out
more information about
Raintree books.

To order:
☎ Phone 0845 6044371
🖹 Fax +44 (0) 1865 312263
📠 Email myorders@raintreepublishers.co.uk

Customers from outside the UK please telephone +44 1865 312262

Raintree is an imprint of Capstone Global Library
Limited, a company incorporated in England and Wales
having its registered office at 7 Pilgrim Street, London,
EC4V 6LB – Registered company number: 6695582

Edited by Louise Galpine and Laura Knowles
Designed by Philippa Jenkins
Original illustrations © Capstone Global Library
    Limited 2012
Picture research by Mica Brancic
Originated by Capstone Global Library Limited
Printed and bound in China by CTPS

ISBN 978 1 406 22269 2 (hardback)
15 14 13 12 11
10 9 8 7 6 5 4 3 2 1

ISBN 978 1 406 22276 0 (paperback)
16 15 14 13 12
10 9 8 7 6 5 4 3 2 1

British Library Cataloguing in Publication Data
Spilsbury, Louise.
The radio. -- (Tales of invention)
621.3'8418'09-dc22
A full catalogue record for this book is available from
the British Library.

Acknowledgements
We would like to thank the following for permission
to reproduce photographs: Alamy pp. 4 (© Image
Source/IE040), 17 (© Mary Evans Picture Library), 21
(© Edward Simons), 22 (© Kuttig - RF – Kids); Corbis
pp. 5 (© Underwood & Underwood), 8 (© Bettmann),
11 (© Bettmann), 12 (© Underwood & Underwood),
15 (© Bettmann), 18 (© Bettmann), 19 (© Sunset
Boulevard), 20 (ClassicStock/© H. Armstrong Roberts),
23 (© Simon Jarratt), 25 (© Douglas Keister), 27
(Reuters/© STR/Shapi Shacinda); Getty Images
pp. 6 (Science & Society Picture Library), 10 (Hulton
Archive), 24 (Photodisc/StockTrek); The Art Archive
p. 14 (Culver Pictures).

Cover photograph of early morning workers in a New
York diner listen to the broadcast of Princess Elizabeth's
wedding in London, November 20, 1947 reproduced with
permission of Corbis/© Bettmann.

We would like to thank Walter Podrazik for his
invaluable help in the preparation of this book.

Every effort has been made to contact copyright holders
of material reproduced in this book. Any omissions will
be rectified in subsequent printings if notice is given to
the publisher.

CONTENTS

Look for these boxes

Biographies

These boxes tell you about the life of inventors, the dates when they lived, and their important discoveries.

Setbacks

Here we tell you about the experiments that didn't work, the failures, and the accidents.

EUREKA!

These boxes tell you about important events and discoveries, and what inspired them.

Any words appearing in the text in bold, **like this**, are explained in the glossary.

TIMELINE

2011 – The timeline shows you when important discoveries and inventions were made.

RADIO TODAY

Millions of people around the world listen to the radio every day. Some listen to up-to-date local or world news. Others swap opinions on radio call-in shows. Radio entertainment includes music of different styles and live sport commentaries, but radio **broadcasts** can also be important for work and safety. For example, radio shipping reports tell sailors where there are rough seas.

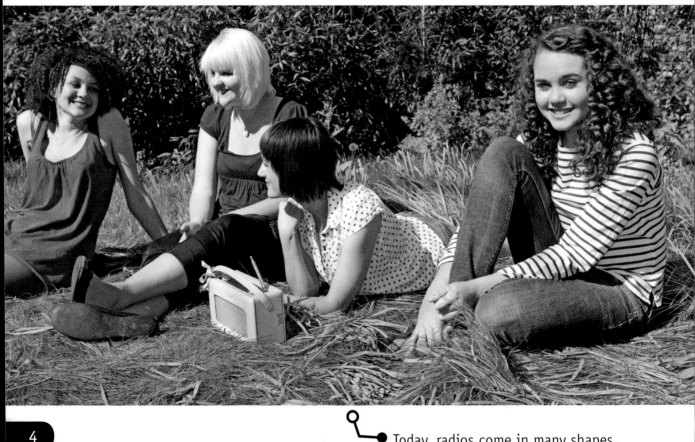

Today, radios come in many shapes, sizes, and colours. Have you ever thought about how a radio works?

1837 – Samuel Morse invents the telegraph

1835   1840

Before radio, wires strung between poles were the quickest way to send information such as news over long distances.

Before radio

The radios we listen to receive signals that carry information through the air. Before radio, messages could only be sent long distances as signals through wires, for example in early **telegraph** and telephone systems. These were limited by how far the wires extended, and messages could only be carried from one person to another. This meant that news spread much more slowly than today.

The invention of the radio – or "wireless" as it was once known – took many people years to develop and improve. The radio allowed people to listen to the same broadcasts straight away and in many places, far from where the signals were sent.

5

Scottish scientist James Clerk Maxwell had the idea that **radio waves** existed in the 1860s. However, it wasn't until 1888 that German physics professor Heinrich Hertz proved this was true. Hertz made sparks of **electricity** jump across a gap between two metal rods, causing pulses of electricity in another machine a short distance away. He proved that electrical energy could be made and **transmitted** through the air in radio waves. If radio waves could carry energy, perhaps they could be used to send information.

Heinrich Hertz was one of the first people to demonstrate radio waves and to imagine the possibilities of radio technology.

Setbacks

Unfortunately, Hertz was not a well man. He died at the age of 36, before anyone invented a radio that used his ideas.

1850   1855

What are radio waves?

We cannot see radio waves, but they are **vibrations** carrying energy. There are many different kinds of similar waves moving through air or space. They include microwaves used for cooking food, the light waves in sunlight, and the X-rays we use to see inside bodies.

These waves travel very fast and straight with a regular up-and-down movement, rather like ocean waves. The amount of energy they carry varies by **amplitude** (the height of the wave), **wavelength** (the gap between tips of waves), and **frequency** (the number of waves that go past a certain point each second). Frequency is measured with a unit called a hertz, in honour of Heinrich Hertz.

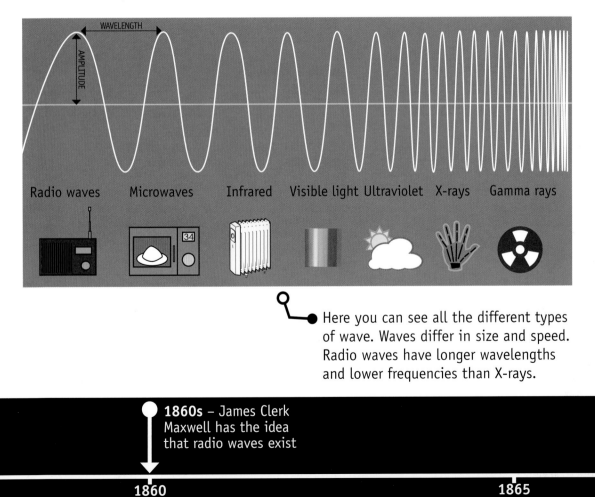

Here you can see all the different types of wave. Waves differ in size and speed. Radio waves have longer wavelengths and lower frequencies than X-rays.

1860s – James Clerk Maxwell has the idea that radio waves exist

1860   1865

Sending waves

Many scientists began to build on Hertz's work to send radio waves further. In 1891, Serbian engineer Nikola Tesla made a **device** that produced and transmitted high-frequency electricity. It was called a Tesla coil. By adding an **antenna** to the coil, Tesla could use the electricity to transmit radio waves to another coil over a distance of 45 kilometres (30 miles). By 1898, Tesla was also using radio waves to control the motor on a model boat!

Early examples of Tesla's coil made large, beautiful sparks of electricity!

Receiving waves

The piece of equipment that sends a radio wave is called a **transmitter**. The part that receives it is a **receiver**. British scientist Oliver Lodge perfected a device he called a "**coherer**", to make receivers better at detecting radio waves.

The coherer was a glass tube with **iron filings** inside. These cohered (clumped) together when radio waves passed through them, then separated again. In 1894, Lodge claimed that he had used his coherer to receive a radio signal around 800 metres (2,625 feet) away from a transmitter.

A transmitter with an antenna can send energy through the air as radio waves to a receiver.

radio waves

antenna

antenna

transmitter

receiver

1875

1880

THE FIRST RADIO?

Italian scientist Guglielmo Marconi realized that to send signals across very long distances, you need a very high aerial, or **antenna**. This meant the signals could travel in straight lines without being blocked by buildings, hills, or other objects. In 1899, Marconi sent **radio waves** across the English Channel. Then, in 1901 he became the first person to send a **transatlantic** message using **Morse Code**. He sent it from Cornwall, England to Newfoundland. Marconi was the first person to show the world how practical radio could be for communication.

In 1901, Marconi tried to use a balloon to hold an antenna high in the air. But when winds blew it away he used a kite about 70 metres (230 feet) high in the sky to send the first transatlantic **broadcast** instead.

Marconi and his team relied on kites to make the first radio broadcast possible.

1888 – Heinrich Hertz proves electrical energy can be transmitted in radio waves (see page 6)

1880   1885

The power of patents

Marconi held the first valid **patent** for radio. A patent is official proof that someone has invented something new so that other people cannot copy it without permission. In fact, many people claimed to have invented radio first but did not bother to get patents or other proof of their achievements! These people included Russian Alexander Popov, who **transmitted** and received radio waves in 1895, and Indian J.C. Bose who transmitted signals over 1.6 kilometres (1 mile) in 1896. Other people claim that pioneers Tesla and Lodge were really the inventors of radio because their ideas were used by Marconi.

This is Marconi's first radio. Was Marconi the real "father of radio", or just a better businessman than the other inventors?

1891 – Nikola Tesla makes a **device** to produce and transmit high **frequency electricity** (see page 8)

1894 – Oliver Lodge makes a **coherer** to receive a radio signal 800 metres (2,625 feet) away (see page 9)

1895 – Alexander Popov transmits and receives radio waves in Russia

1890 1895

1895 – Marconi sends radio waves across a room

1896 – Indian scientist J.C. Bose transmits radio signals over 1.6 kilometres (1 mile) (see page 11)

1898 – Tesla builds a radio-controlled model boat (see page 8)

1899 – Marconi sends radio waves across the English Channel

1900 – Reginald Fessenden sends the first voice signals by radio over a short distance (see page 16)

1895

1900

Guglielmo Marconi (1874–1937)

Guglielmo Marconi became interested in **electricity** as a schoolchild. Later, he turned two rooms in his family's home in Italy into laboratories where he carried out experiments. It is believed that in 1895 Marconi managed to send radio waves from a **transmitter** at one end of a room to a **receiver** that then rang a bell at the other end. He soon adapted this **device** to send messages in Morse code.

When the Italian government showed no interest in his invention, Marconi and his mother moved to England and set up their own company. This company applied for patents across the world and organized events to get publicity. For example, in 1898 they installed a radio on Queen Victoria's yacht so she could send messages from land to her son on board. By the early 1900s, Marconi's radio invention was being used in many places around the world. For his achievements, Marconi was awarded the 1909 Nobel Prize for Physics.

During World War I, Marconi returned to Italy where he was in charge of wireless **telegraph** communication for the army. Then in 1931, to celebrate the 30th anniversary of his first transatlantic message, he spoke in a radio broadcast. When he died in 1937, radio stations around the world stopped transmitting for a short period of silence during his funeral.

1901 – Marconi sends the first transatlantic radio message (see page 10)

1906 – Reginald Fessenden sends voice signals several hundred kilometres (see page 16)

1909 – Marconi is awarded the Nobel Prize for Physics

1905

1910

Using early radios

The first radios could only send messages by Morse Code. They were mostly used for communication between ships and land, because places on land continued to use wired telegraph systems. Using Morse Code, ships could receive news and weather reports and call for help if they needed it.

In written Morse Code, letters of the alphabet are shown as dots and dashes. To send the code by radio, transmitters are switched on and off to make short and long signals. For example, the international distress signal SOS ...---... was sent as three short, three long, and three short pulses by radio.

In the early 1900s, all new ships had radios for safety and skilled radio operators were vital on land and at sea.

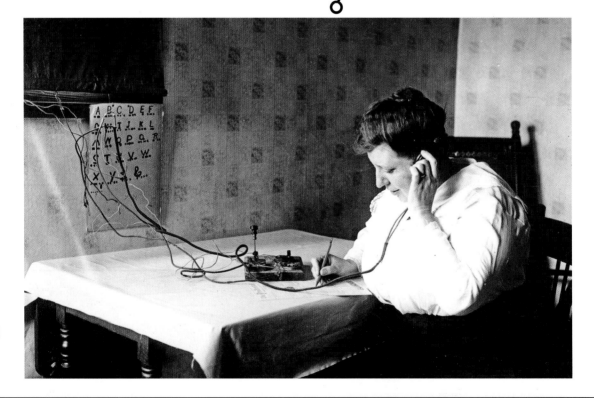

1910 – Murderer Dr Crippen is caught because of radio

1912 – Radio distress calls from the *Titanic* save 700 people's lives

1910

1915

The tragedy of the *Titanic* proved to the world the importance of radios for safety on ships.

Radio rescue

In 1912, the luxury ocean liner *Titanic* was on its first voyage when it hit an iceberg and began to sink. There were 2,200 passengers and crew on board. The two Marconi company radio operators on board sent distress calls in Morse Code to nearby ships. Their use of radio allowed 700 people to be rescued.

EUREKA!

In 1910, Dr Crippen murdered his wife and fled London with his girlfriend on a slow ship bound for Canada. The captain became suspicious of Crippen's behaviour because the girlfriend was disguised as a boy. He used the ship's radio to inform the police, who by then had discovered Crippen's wife's body. The police got on a faster ship and arrested Crippen for the crime before he could escape to Canada.

15

1920 – The first public radio broadcasting station is opened in the United States (see page 17)

WIRELESS WORLD

The next big invention after sending **Morse Code** signals was to **broadcast** the human voice. Canadian engineer Reginald Fessenden first did this in 1900, but his voice only travelled a few metres. Fessenden set up a powerful **transmitter**, with a microphone connected, that produced a steady radio signal from an aerial. The changing pattern of electrical signals made by the microphone as he spoke into it caused the **radio waves** to increase. Radio **receivers** have **loudspeakers** that convert radio wave signals back into sound.

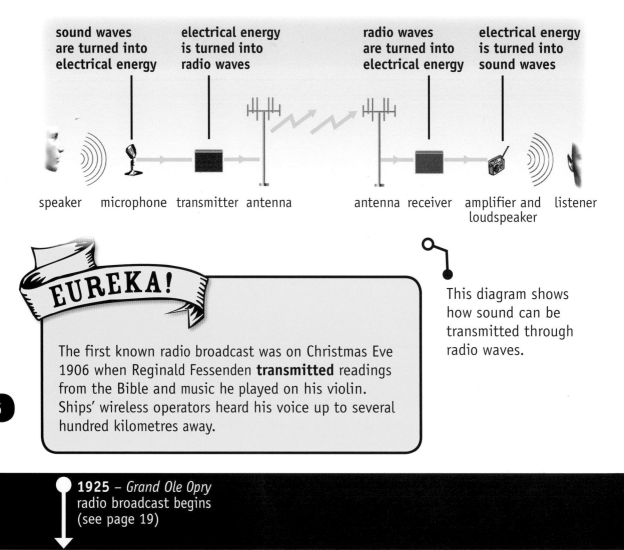

| sound waves are turned into electrical energy | electrical energy is turned into radio waves | radio waves are turned into electrical energy | electrical energy is turned into sound waves |

speaker   microphone transmitter antenna   antenna receiver amplifier and   listener
                                                                         loudspeaker

This diagram shows how sound can be transmitted through radio waves.

EUREKA!

The first known radio broadcast was on Christmas Eve 1906 when Reginald Fessenden **transmitted** readings from the Bible and music he played on his violin. Ships' wireless operators heard his voice up to several hundred kilometres away.

1925 – *Grand Ole Opry* radio broadcast begins (see page 19)

1925   1930

Radios at war

During World War I (1914–1918), all work on radio development focused on its use in battle. In the United Kingdom, the government took control of the Marconi Company and began training new operators. All armies and navies in the war used radio to pass on orders and communications. Radio could also be used to locate enemy transmitters in order to plan attacks.

Public broadcasts

After the war, more people had heard about and wanted to use this amazing new technology. In 1920 Marconi started broadcasting music to the public. The first radio broadcasting station aimed at the general public opened in the United States in the same year. Other stations soon followed, at first mostly broadcasting talk and music.

Here, German soldiers are using a mobile radio station during World War I.

1937 – The first radio telescope is made (see page 24)

1935   1940

The Radio Age

The 1920s and 1930s were a boom time for radio. People rushed to buy new radios with inbuilt **speakers** that the whole family could listen to together. Hundreds of radio stations broadcast on different **frequencies**. People turned the dials on their receivers to find particular frequencies, or kept turning until they heard something of interest.

In the United States, between 1923 and 1930, 60 per cent of US families bought radio receivers!

1940 – Hedy Lamarr invents a way of fooling enemy radio-tracking systems

1940   1945

EUREKA!

In November 1925, a radio station in Nashville, USA, started to broadcast a show named *Grand Ole Opry*. The show featured performances of American folk music in front of live audiences. By the 1930s, it was so popular it had to move to a larger studio. Today, *Grand Ole Opry* is the longest running radio show in history.

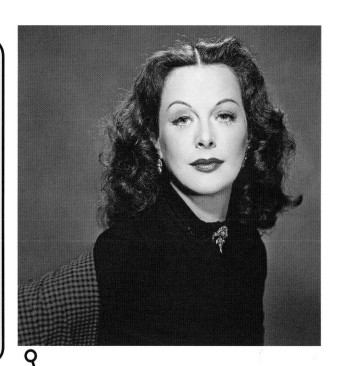

Hedy Lamarr invented a way to stop the Nazis in World War II from receiving radio broadcasts to the US troops.

World War II

During World War II, radio became an important tool for people to hear war news, warnings of attacks, and **propaganda** from their leaders. Throughout Germany, loudspeakers put up in streets broadcast messages from the Nazi leader Adolf Hitler. Radio was also used by armed forces to defend against the enemy. Signals from radios could be used to detect an enemy's hiding place.

In the 1940s, radio signals used to control US torpedoes were being tracked and jammed by Nazis. American film star Hedy Lamarr realized the signals would be impossible to jam if transmitters and receivers rapidly switched frequencies. Only operators who knew the sequence of frequencies could unjumble the messages. Lamarr's "frequency hopping" idea was ignored at first, but was eventually used by the army in the 1960s – and recently in mobile phones!

19

1954 – The first **transistor** radio goes on sale (see pages 20 and 21)

1950   1955

Portable radios

Early radios had large **valves**. These were special glass tubes that **amplified** sound signals so sound could be heard through a loudspeaker. This meant that early radios were big and bulky. In 1948, the **transistor** was invented independently by two German scientists, Herbert Mataré and Heinrich Welker. Transistors did the same job as the valves, but they were much smaller.

Pop stations

In the 1960s, countries such as the United Kingdom and Denmark mostly broadcast music that was recorded by the radio station's own orchestras. Then several independent radio stations started broadcasting just the pop records that young people liked. Some set up outside of countries, as they had no official permission to broadcast. These were known as pirate radio stations. Radio Caroline transmitted to teenagers in the United Kingdom from ships in the North Sea!

Small transistor radios were powered with small batteries so they could be carried around and listened to anywhere.

Digital radio

Digital radio was developed in the 1990s by a group of European radio broadcasters and manufacturers. With this system, a transmitter sends fragments of signals as a code made up of numbers. The receiver pieces together the codes into a complete signal. There are several advantages over earlier radio signals. Digital signals have less **interference** (crackling sound). As well as sound, text and images can also be packed into the same frequencies.

A digital radio collects coded radio signals from the air, and combines them in order to form uninterrupted sounds.

1964 – Radio Caroline pirate station starts broadcasting

We use **radio waves** and signals for listening to music and voices but also to control many things, from toy robots, cars, and boats to mobile phones and televisions.

How radio control works

How can you use radio waves to control the movement of a toy car? When you press a trigger on a handset, the **transmitter** sends a sequence of electrical pulses as radio waves. The toy car has a **receiver** which searches for signals on that **frequency**. Electronics inside the car decode the pulses to make motors work to move the car. For example, 16 pulses might make a toy car move forward and 40 pulses move it into reverse.

Radio waves can be used to have fun as well as for communication.

EUREKA!

The name *Bluetooth* comes from a Danish Viking king called Bluetooth, who lived in the 900s. King Bluetooth united fighting tribes and the Bluetooth radio link was created to "unite" together lots of different devices!

Bluetooth

In 1998, Ericsson, the Swedish manufacturer of mobile phones, formed a group of electronics companies to produce **devices** that worked using Bluetooth technology. Bluetooth is a special radio link that allows laptop computers, mobile phones, and other fixed and portable devices to transfer data over short distances without being connected by wires. Bluetooth sends sounds and information by radio waves and changes frequency thousands of times a second to avoid radio **interference**.

People often use Bluetooth headsets to speak on mobiles without holding them to their ear.

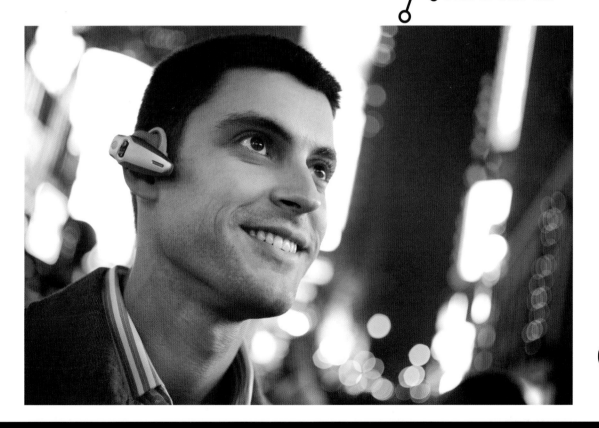

Radio telescopes

Radio waves are also used to detect distant objects in space. Stars, galaxies, and other objects in space naturally give off radio waves. But they are so far away that these signals are very weak when they reach Earth. Radio engineer Grote Reber made the first radio telescope to capture such signals in 1937. Today, radio telescopes have a giant **antenna** to pick up the radio waves, a receiver to **amplify** the signals, and a computer to interpret them.

Some people hope giant dish-shaped antennae on radio telescopes might capture communications from life on distant planets!

In 1931, American radio engineer Karl Jansky could not work out why his radio was crackling. When he pointed the antenna to the sky he realised that radio waves from distant stars were creating interference.

1990s – People are able to use Global Positioning Systems (GPS) to locate positions on Earth

1990s – Digital radio is invented

1991 – The wind-up radio is invented (see page 27)

1985

1990

Radio navigation

The same types of antennae used in radio telescopes are also used to track and collect data from **satellites** in space. In **Global Positioning Systems (GPS)**, radio signals are sent from a network of satellites in space to receivers on the ground. The receivers collect and convert the signals to tell people where they are or where they want to go. The first GPS satellites were meant for army and navy use but by 1993, GPS was being used by ordinary people, too.

In cars, satellite navigation systems, also called "sat navs", use GPS to show drivers which route to take.

1994 – The first Internet radio station is **broadcast** (see page 26)

1998 – Bluetooth wireless communication is invented (see page 23)

1995

2000

Today, radio sets are very different from the early models. They come in many sizes and shapes, can be set into sunglasses or watches, and have access to thousands of programmes. What will radio be like in the future?

Changing broadcasts

In the future, there may not even be separate radio sets any more, as more stations **broadcast** over the Internet to wireless **devices** such as mobile phones or laptops. In 1994, an American radio station called WXYC became the first to broadcast on the Internet. In 2008, Sirius XM formed the largest **satellite** radio service in the world. People pay a monthly fee for a **receiver** and access to radio broadcasts. It has a very high-quality sound and no **interference**.

EUREKA!

In 1991, Trevor Baylis watched a TV programme about the spread of **AIDS** in Africa. It described how difficult it was to tell people how to avoid the disease because people could not afford or did not have electricity to power radios. Baylis went straight to his workshop and made the first wind-up radio using spare parts he found in there.

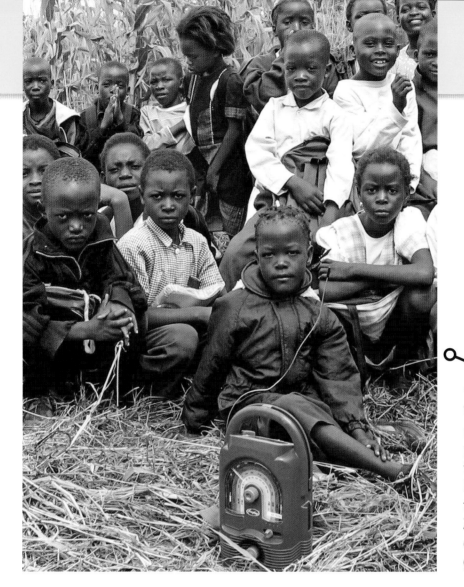

Wind-up radios make their own power. This one is being used to broadcast lessons to children in Zambia who cannot afford to go to school.

Green technology

Making **electricity** to run radios and other machines causes problems like **pollution** and **global warming**. So, people have invented radios that run on other sources of power, such as solar (energy from the Sun), and wind-up radios. These radios are also useful in places where electricity is unavailable, such as after a natural disaster like an earthquake, or in remote parts of the world.

27

2008 – Sirius XM satellite radio service begins to broadcast

TIMELINE

1837
Samuel Morse invents the **telegraph**

1860s
James Clerk Maxwell has the idea that **radio waves** exist

1888
Heinrich Hertz proves electrical energy can be **transmitted** in radio waves

1906
Reginald Fessenden sends voice signals several hundred kilometres

1901
Marconi sends the first **transatlantic** radio message

1900
Reginald Fessenden sends the first voice signals by radio over a short distance

1909
Marconi is awarded the Nobel Prize for Physics

1912
Radio distress calls from the *Titanic* save 700 people's lives

1920
The first public radio **broadcasting** station is opened in the United States

2008
Sirius XM **satellite** radio service begins to broadcast

1998
Bluetooth wireless communication is invented

1994
The first Internet radio station is broadcast

1891
Nikola Tesla makes a **device** to produce and transmit high-**frequency electricity**

1894
Oliver Lodge makes a **coherer** to receive a radio signal 800 metres (2,625 feet) away

1895
Alexander Popov transmits and receives radio waves in Russia. Marconi sends radio waves across a room.

1896
Indian scientist J.C. Bose transmits radio signals over 1.6 kilometres (1 mile)

1898
Tesla builds a radio-controlled model boat

1899
Marconi sends radio waves across the English Channel

1937
The first radio telescope is made

1940
Hedy Lamarr invents a way of fooling enemy radio-tracking systems

1954
The first **transistor** radio goes on sale

1964
Radio Caroline pirate station starts broadcasting

1990s
Digital radio is invented. People are able to use **GPS** to locate positions on Earth.

1991
The wind-up radio is invented

GLOSSARY

AIDS stands for acquired immunodeficiency syndrome; a disease for which there is no known cure. It is most common in African countries.

amplify increase volume of a sound signal

amplitude height of a wave and also a measure of its strength

antenna (plural: antennae) device converting radio signals into electricity and electricity into radio signals

broadcast sending out radio signals from a transmitter for anyone to receive

coherer early device to detect radio signals

device piece of equipment wth a particular purpose

electricity form of energy from the flow of an electric charge

frequency measure of the number of times something, such as a wave peak, passes a point in a given time

Global Positioning System (GPS) instrument that finds a precise position on Earth using radio time signals from satellites

global warming gradual warming of Earth's atmosphere caused mainly by gases released when we burn fuels

interference when obstacles or other radio waves interrupt a radio signal, often causing a crackling sound

iron filings tiny pieces of iron

loudspeaker machine that converts electrical signals into sound waves

Morse Code system of dots and dashes that stand for letters, numbers, and other symbols

patent official proof that an invention, idea, or process was the idea of a particular person, and protection from it being copied

pollution when air, soil, or water is made dirty with harmful substances

propaganda specific ideas or views spread around to influence others. For example, Hitler's propaganda encouraged people to join the Nazi party.

radio wave type of wave used for broadcasting radio signals

receiver device that receives radio signals using an antenna and converts them into sound

satellite man-made object put into space to move around Earth, often to transmit radio and other signals

telegraph system for sending messages by radio waves or electric wires

transatlantic across the Atlantic ocean

transistor device to amplify an electrical signal that can switch on and off

transmit send signals containing information

transmitter device that converts electrical signals into radio waves and sends out the signals

valve early device that acts like a transistor

vibration move rapidly up and down or forwards and backwards

wavelength distance between the peaks of one wave and the next

FIND OUT MORE

Books

Guglielmo Marconi (Atomic) John Malam (Raintree, 2008)

Inventing the Radio (Breakthrough Inventions) Marianne Fedunkiw (Crabtree Publishing, 2007)

Websites

www.fcc.gov/cgb/kidszone/faqs_radio.html
This website answers some common questions about how radios work.

www.nrao.edu/index.php/learn/radioastronomy/radiocommunication
Go to this website to find out more about sound and radio waves.

www.classbraingames.com/2009/12/learn-morse-code/
Visit this website to learn Morse Code.

Places to visit

The Museum of Communication
131 High Street, Burntisland
Fife KY3 9AA
www.mocft.co.uk

National Media Museum
Bradford, West Yorkshire, BD1 1NQ
www.nationalmediamuseum.org.uk

Science Museum
South Kensington, London, SW7 2DD
www.sciencemuseum.org.uk

INDEX